There is a Light at the End of the Tunnel

(Photo: Marie Claire, June 2005)

Airlie Jane Kirkham

There is a Light at the End of the Tunnel

Acknowledgements

Thanks are extended to all who have helped
in the production of this book.

To my mother, who has been my amanuensis, my
guiding light and support throughout the many
years it has taken to complete this story.

To my many friends who have read my poems and given me good
feedback – Margaret, Freda, Barbara, Deb, and many others.

To my mentors in this project – Rev. Dawn Colsey and
members of the Poets of Passion Poetry Group; Jules Leigh
Koch, a member of Friendly Street Poets; Alison McDonald;
and Amelia Walker my cousin, who also writes poetry.

To Bridget McDonald, who has advised me on editing and layout.

To those unnamed who have assisted in any other ways.

There is a Light at the End of the Tunnel
ISBN 978 1 76041 405 4
Copyright © text Airlie Jane Kirkham 2017
Internal photos by Pamela Margaret Kirkham unless otherwise stated
Front cover photo: Pamela Margaret Kirkham
Back cover photo: Bryan Charlton

First published 2017 by
GINNINDERRA PRESS
PO Box 3461 Port Adelaide 5015
www.ginninderrapress.com.au

Contents

Foreword	7
Prologue: Courage and Faith	9
Introduction	11
1 Early Years	13
2 Teaching at Saints	17
3 Redirected Lives	18
4 A Miracle	24
5 Letters from Prison	30
6 Awakenings	34
7 Hopes and Aspirations	44
8 Thoughts and Feelings	54
9 Support from Others	58
10 Helping Others	62
11 Life at Home	66
12 A Dream Come True	72
Epilogue	81

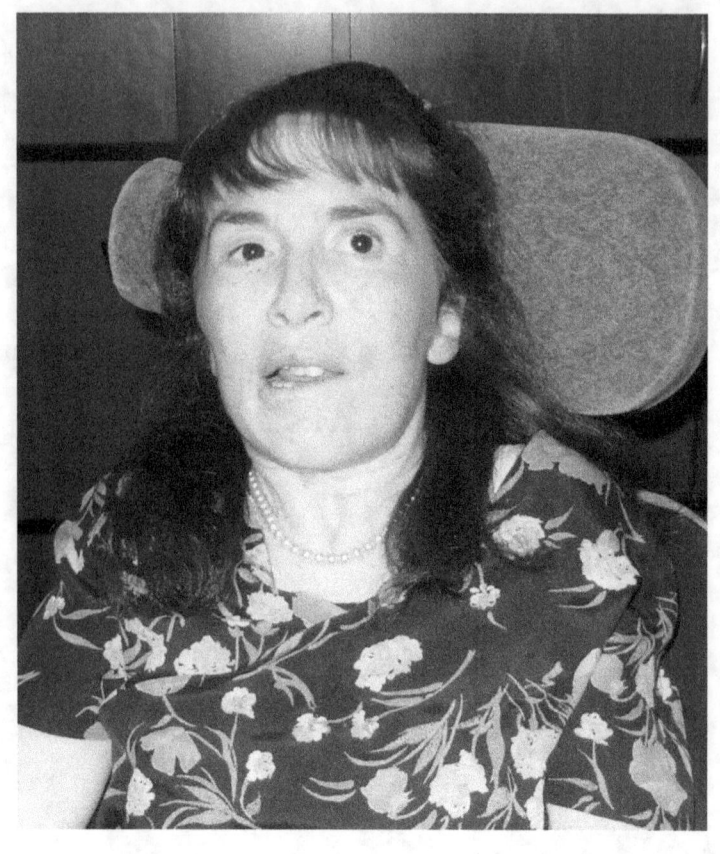

Foreword

Words cannot describe my longing to write my book - a light at the end of a very long tunnel / A glimpse a pin prick of light will enhance my thoughts and feelings like those miners who have longed for daylight.
Now I can see the way more clearly
Obstacles are becoming soft and pliable, like moulding dough.
I want the world to know my story
It is a simple story life after near death after all I had was taken from me except my breath
one lr thing that was not taken was my faith in God ——— my time memory For this I am thankful

My book
will soon be real.
Words, thoughts,
poetry, prose.
My book will reveal much.
My experiences,
my journey along
this difficult road.
My book will create thought,
discussion, controversy,
masterful ideas, dreams
which have come true.
My book, above all,
will testify my faith in God
who has stood by me
these long years.

Passion
Patience
Persistence
Perseverance
Perspiration

Prologue: Courage and Faith

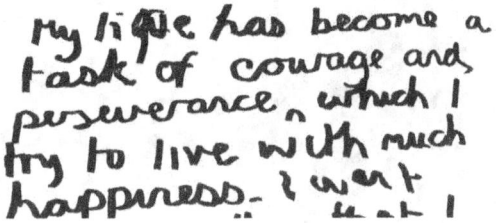

My life has become a task of courage and perseverance which I try to live with much happiness. I want to show others that I am able to be courageous, and persevere towards my goal of being warden of myself. I have had a very strong faith in God who has helped me to overcome my problems, and for my family who have stood by me courageously too.

My courage has made me determined to succeed and I hope I can achieve this. My aim is to be a person who can show others how to persevere and try to be courageous when they have some trouble or have an accident. I had an accident, and now I can't do many, many things, but I am able to write about courage and perseverance. We can make the best out of a situation by being courageous and my strong faith that God will look after me. We can make ourselves courageous by being more positive in our daily race with life and try to be more masterful in all we do, when we make many decisions.

I have tried to be courageous when I have had to have operations and injections, so I know my limitation and difficulties when I have any trouble. My main aim is to encourage others to not give up when things are not going well. We must continue with more courage because we can do all things through Christ which strengthens me (Philippians 4:13).

*This was written 30 July 1997,
for the John Dunne Awards at Julia Farr Services.*

Introduction

Thomas Hardy once said, 'A tale must be exceptional enough to justify its telling.'

I think my story is exceptional. Maybe you will think so too. Whatever one thinks, I have learnt through this story the value of persistence, patience, positive attitude and perseverance – such precious qualities in life.

Poem – Myself as an Author

My mind is working overtime.
I am in a mood full of ideas
for my book.

Writing is a pleasure.
It is enjoyable to read
a story of courage,
perseverance, patience
and persistence.

Who will read my story?
Those who are curious, sceptical, interested,
caring people who have shared my journey
along this difficult road.

I want to sing for joy,
rejoice, praise God
for His renewed gift to me
of communication in this medium.

Above all,
my book will testify
my faith in God, who has stood by me
these long years.

My book will allow
people to reflect
on life and all its mysteries:
its good time, its tragedies.
Take nothing for granted again.

28 November 1999

This is my tale, which needs to be told.

I was born in Adelaide on Thursday 21 October 1965 to Pamela Margaret Kirkham (née Donaldson) and Leslie James Kirkham. My family lived at Lockleys, and I, together with my younger sister Katrina Leanne Rycroft (née Kirkham), attended Lockleys North Primary School for seven years.

During that time, I was a keen member of the local Girl Guide group, at first as a Brownie, and subsequently as a Guide and Ranger Guide. I attended Holy Trinity Church, participated in the Sunday school, youth groups and played netball.

1
Early Years

Primary school days

When I was two and a half years old, I started kindergarten at the Lady Gowrie Child Centre, Thebarton, and at five years, I started primary school at Lockleys North. I took to school like a duck to water. I loved it. My greatest love was learning to read. I became an avid reader and my reading age was always well beyond my years. I loved books and writing. When I was about ten, the school told Mum I had a reading age of sixteen-plus years. I was rather shy as a child, and just loved being a bookworm, reading by myself.

At school, I made many friends. Felicity, Belinda, Alison and Pat were my closest friends but I don't see any of them now. Felicity lived two doors away in my street and we walked to school each day until we were old enough to ride our bikes. We went on camps and to concerts. I remember going on a school camp with Mr Peter Carter. He was a canoeing expert, who also taught us maths and science, and he took our class to a bush camp on Eyre Peninsula near Port Lincoln. There were no bathrooms there at the campsite so he simply told us to jump into the sea for our ablutions, and find a bush for other necessities. I am sure my mother would not have approved, nor the school for that matter. Rules are much tighter these days for children's safety. I remember most of my teachers with affection, especially Mr Errey. He was a good teacher and used to make us laugh a lot. I enjoyed my time there and did well at primary school.

When we were young, Mum and Dad used to take us to Melbourne by car to visit our grandparents and great aunt. We would always call at Keilor on the way in to Melbourne to see Auntie Alma for afternoon tea, which was usually Dad's favourite gooseberry pie and cream. One time, she had a large feather and she used it to tickle me and have a laugh, hoping I would laugh too. But I hated it and from then on grew my great hatred of feathers lasting to this day. Whenever I was naughty, Mum would say, 'Shall I get the feather out?' and I would run a mile from the feather to escape punishment. Today, I don't hate feathers quite so much any more.

Katrina and I played netball for the local Uniting Church team for a few years. One day in 1978, we were waiting on the footpath on Henley Beach Road for Dad to pick us up after the match. We were playing around with our netball when it accidentally rolled on to the road. Foolishly, I rushed out to get it, not noticing an approaching car, which was unable to stop in time. Fortunately, I broke only my leg, but I ended up in hospital. It was in the days before mobile phones, so poor Mum was home wondering why Dad hadn't arrived with two passengers. They were all at the Queen Elizabeth Hospital. That was my first brush with hospital life and plasters, which much later were to dominate my life.

Life at Woodlands 1978–1982

When I was in year seven, I won a scholarship to Woodlands Church of England Girls Grammar School, Glenelg. I was very happy, as my mum had won this award too. I started in 1978 in year eight. I loved it from the start. I was keen to learn languages, so I took French and Japanese. I did well in those, so I continued them right to matriculation level. In year ten, in 1980, I won the Elaine Balfour-Ogilvy Scholarship, awarded to the daughter of an old scholar. I felt specially honoured.

I enjoyed other subjects but most of all music. I had been learning piano since I was five, and in year eight, I started learning the violin. Later I completed grade eight piano with honours. I joined the school choir, as I loved singing. I was also in the orchestra, playing violin, my second instrument. In year twelve, I was elected leader of the choir, a position

I had always coveted. As well, I entered the annual music competitions and won several. I was also awarded a school blue for music.

I wasn't really a sports person, but played hockey and netball. I had my front tooth knocked out playing hockey when I was in year ten. A girl broke the rule of sticks and hit my mouth with her raised stick. I liked chess better, and my friend Cathy and I virtually ran the chess club at that time. We entered all the inter-school contests. I won a certificate for winning more than eighty per cent of my games and a school blue for chess.

During this time, I was a keen member of the local Girl Guide group, earning my BP Peak Achievement badge; later I was a Ranger Guide.

We had great fun at school and we had some wonderful teachers and school chaplain, Rev. Stewart Langshaw. They nurtured in me my love of learning, of books and knowledge, which has lasted me all my life. In 1982, I won second prize in the poetry section of the inaugural Young Writers' Award (SA).

University years 1984–1991

I left school in 1982, having done very well in my matriculation exam. I wanted to be a teacher of Japanese, English and Music. I decided to do an Arts degree. My time at Adelaide University was some of my happiest years. I met lots of new friends whom I cherished for their fun and the good times we had together. I am not sure how much studying we did but I managed to graduate in 1986 with a Bachelor of Arts. During the last years of my Arts degree, I decided to complete a Music degree as well, with some cross-crediting of subjects. The next year I did my Graduate Diploma of Education, which included many practical teaching sessions in schools to develop my teaching skills, and went on further with my music.

After I finished my degree, I travelled to Japan for two months with a Japanese Language Association scholarship to study the language and culture. I had a happy and very satisfying life. I enjoyed music and friendships.

Interim Teaching Report

9/3/87

Miss A. Kirkham

Class: English 1029.

Miss Kirkham has made a sound beginning in her teaching of class 1029.

Lessons are very well prepared. The lessons have a sense of direction and there is a pleasing variety of activity.

Miss Kirkham presents herself well in class. Voice and manner are good; questioning is good; eye contact is very good.

Discipline is an area of concern. Miss Kirkham must be vigorous enough to stamp her personality on the class. The class is basically cooperative in comparison with some classes that any teacher will inevitably meet. I feel that confidence in this area is growing but Miss Kirkham must exude a greater sense of mastery.

However, a lot of this comes with experience, and in general to this point Miss Kirkham's teaching practice has been successful.

D.L Rosie.

One of my teaching reports, 1987.

2
Teaching at Saints

I started to teach Japanese at Saint Peter's Collegiate Girls' School in 1988. I loved teaching there, and I gradually introduced the language throughout the school, adding a new year level each year. We had lots of fun playing shops (in Japanese of course) with the junior students, and performing small plays which the students had written. At the same time, little by little, I enrolled in the required units, completing my music degree, Bachelor of Music, in 1991.

I had normally been a quiet, reserved person, but in this my first teaching position, I learnt to be outgoing and entered into the life of the school. In August 1991, just before my accident, we had an exchange visit from a school in Japan. My family and I hosted a Japanese student for two weeks. This was a great time of cultural exchange for my Japanese classes at Saints. I would have continued to teach Japanese at Saints if I had not had my accident.

But to carry on at Saints was not to be.

3

Redirected Lives

Early in 1992, Mum and Dad were asked to write an article about my accident for our church magazine. I had had an accident while driving Mum's car to a friend's kitchen tea at Balaklava. After that, from 29 September 1991, the day of my accident, they had been too worried and busy to do any more than look after me while I was in the Royal Adelaide Hospital and later Julia Farr. They will tell you the story of the first five or six months, because I don't remember very much of that time.

In 'Redirected Lives', *Trinity Times* 1992, Holy Trinity Church Adelaide, Mum and Dad (Pamela and Les) wrote,

> The message light glowed red in the dark as we returned to our Hong Kong Hotel room after our evening meal. They said simply, 'Ring your sister in Australia. It's urgent.'
>
> And so what started out as a simple holiday visiting friends turned into new directions in our lives. Our loved elder daughter, Airlie Jane, was severely injured in a car accident while we were away. All through that long sleepless night as we prayed for her life, the words of the song 'The steadfast love of the Lord never ceases. His mercies never come to an end' kept coming into our minds.
>
> We were sick with shock as we tried to pray, but the Lord did not fail us. The next day as we were finalising our plans to return home, He sent comfort to us in the form of a missionary, whom we had not previously met, living in Hong Kong at the time, but who was related to Adelaide friends. He came to our hotel room as we waited to catch our plane back to Australia. He prayed with us that God would support us through this terrible time, giving us hope, encouragement and strength through God's Word. God knew we needed someone in a strange land.

God heard our prayers and Airlie's life was saved, but then began the long road to try to recover her former self. There must be a reason God saved her life. We looked daily to see what God wanted us to do in this situation. Airlie has suffered greatly; she has tolerated more than anyone can imagine. Every little step of progress Airlie has made has been an answer to a prayer. God has urged us to trust him. We do not know why this burden has been placed upon us, but we do know that God has challenged and strengthened our faith, our prayer and our physical capacity to bear the burden.

As we recollect the two months in the RAH, we recall thinking about the adjustments we would need to make to restore Airlie to the best we could, and provide for her future. From thereon, we had daily visits to her bedside, playing her music and talking to her, assisting in any therapy provided and asking many questions. This was a tiresome journey: at the close of each day we would call in at Trinity on our way home and pray with our Rector for guidance and restoration. No words can describe the feelings we endured, the pain, and tiredness. The neurologist just said, almost daily, 'Wait and see.'

God has kept us free from sickness, He has taken away our tiredness, and He has provided friends and helpers to support and help us carry out therapy with Airlie. All manner of kindnesses and compassion have emerged from this tragedy. We have learnt to care for the system we find ourselves in, to work for better conditions and therapy, for better management of the rehabilitation of the individual. We have met so many new people – nurses, therapists and administrators; we have been able to share those experiences with other families in similar situations. Ideas can often open more doors and we could help each other. Above all, we have had opportunities to witness for the gospel, to tell others how we were strengthened by our faith in God through Jesus Christ, His son.

One day a nurse asked us to explain the Bible verse on Airlie's bedside calendar, 'With God, all things are possible' (Matthew 19:26).

Another asked why Airlie had so many visitors. We explained they were our church friends.

We still do not know why this happened to a high achiever and talented young person like Airlie. Of one thing we are sure. Airlie loved the Lord and she is with Him in spirit though she cannot express it verbally. She responds very positively to the reading of Bible verses and prayer, and to church services which she attends when possible.

As we have expended energy, so Airlie has made progress down the long road to recovery. She was a very articulate young person, but now cannot communicate in a normal manner. Our lives have been redirected, not in the way we would have chosen. We are all being tested as we walk the road to the light at the end of the tunnel.

While Airlie was in the RAH, the hospital chaplain alerted us to a book, *The Catastrophe of Coma: A Way Back*, written by Dr. Ted A. Freeman. We read it from cover to cover, and found it most helpful.

As Malcolm G. MacKay AM, BA, BD, PhD (Chairman Brain Injury Division, Australian Brain Foundation, Canberra) says in the foreword to Ted's book, 'Have faith, hope, and love. Without them, no therapy can heal the person. They are the very lifeblood of human existence. The greatest of them all is love – and the most powerful.'

We followed Ted's suggestions, and set about organising a program for bringing back Airlie's awareness of her environment; as well, we added ideas of our own in a devised plan of stimulation and rehabilitation. Many of our friends joined the team of people who came daily to help us develop this plan. And it worked.

Now just close your eyes, and imagine Airlie herself is telling you her story.

'Let me introduce myself.

I am Airlie Jane Kirkham. I was a language teacher at St Peter's Collegiate Girls School. Driving my car along a country road nearly twenty years ago, in 1991, when I was twenty-five years old, I was driving Mum's car and collided with another car going the other way. I had lost my way and somehow found myself on an unknown dirt road. I had a tragic accident. I don't know how it happened because I can't remember, but Mum tells me the police said I was not speeding. I was taken to a small local country hospital by some off-duty St John's men. I was retrieved from there by helicopter and taken to the Royal Adelaide Hospital. Fancy that. It was my first and only ride in a helicopter and I don't remember a thing about it!

In my accident, I injured part of my brain, had several broken bones and my spleen was removed as it had ruptured. I was in a coma for several weeks. Mum told me later my Glasgow Coma Scale was 4 out of 15, which was not a good sign for recovery. As a result, I was not expected to live. But I did. Now I am unable to walk or talk. However, I can write and think, so I will tell you my story as I remember it.

I have vague memories of intensive care. I remember my parents talking to me and the doctors testing me with pins to see if I could respond. Apart from that, I can't remember very much. Mum told me later that I responded when the doctor told me to breathe. Someone was calling out to me, 'Breathe, Airlie. Breathe. Take a deep breath,' so I did. This was after an episode when I stopped breathing. So right from the beginning, I had some degree of awareness. I did survive, and I feel sure this was because so many people prayed to God for my life to be saved.

Coming out of the coma, I was very sleepy, but I remember being in the Royal Adelaide Hospital for many weeks. My parents sat by my bedside every day and night; many friends prayed for my recovery and visited me with the aim of trying to rouse me. I remember a few of them, especially the Saint Peter's School Chaplain, who came and prayed over me. As I was a teacher at his school, he supported me as well as my parents. Our church pastor, Rev. Reg Piper, did likewise. Every night, Mum and Dad would go home, rather weary but pleased that I was slowly improving.

It was the beginning of a long hard road for everyone, but slowly I have improved. I wasn't in pain, I was sedated so much. It was a period of post-traumatic amnesia. Post-traumatic amnesia (PTA) is a state of confusion that occurs immediately following a traumatic brain injury (TBI) in which the injured person is disoriented and unable to remember events that occur after the injury. It took me a long time to emerge from this. When I was well enough, I was transferred to the Julia Farr Centre for post-accident treatment, where I spent the first six years of my recovery and rehabilitation.

My recollections of Julia Farr are fading. I recall big wards, many people who rushed around looking too busy to be friendly. The rooms were full of people like me, accident victims who were unable to do more than endure the passing of time.

Daily routine was paramount. We could only respond to a timetable. Oh, how I hated being woken at the crack of dawn! I was always tired. People came and went. Nurses came and went, some looking smart in their crisp white uniforms, others wearing a hotch potch of 'civvies'. Often I didn't know who was who. I was totally reliant on nursing staff for daily care, and the quality of such care became crucial to my basic comfort and well-being.

The evenings were the worst. My time seemed to drag. There was little to do except watch TV and I couldn't see that properly, even if I'd been interested in the soapy programs they put on. I was often in the back row of chairs and my eyes weren't functioning properly either. They put us to bed so early. How could we complain? Few of us could talk. I longed for the morning when action began. Mum and Dad came to help me during the day with my meals and drinks, exercises and toilet, and when various therapies such as physio and occupational therapy took place. It relieved the monotony of a dreary place where nothing happens except meals, medication and bed.

At times, people would come and talk over me, not to me. Many thought I was vegetative, because I could not communicate or respond, or even move a muscle. I could move my right leg a bit but that was all at that time. I felt locked in because I couldn't speak or even write. The locked-in state is a diagnosis applied to people who demonstrate alertness and wakefulness but who cannot respond by talking or moving a muscle.

I could see everything and everyone. I knew who they were. I could hear the people talking about me and saying things I didn't like. I wasn't asked if I wanted to do something. I would have liked people to talk to me properly as I could hear and understand, but they didn't believe I could, so they didn't bother. I could smell OK. I could smell the various smells coming from different rooms on my ward – the pantry, the dining room, the pan room!

I felt very frustrated, at times angry, because often no one would come near me nor talk to me, only Mum and Dad, my visitors or therapists. I was frustrated because I couldn't make decisions, or tell people what I wanted. I wasn't in control of myself. I learnt to wriggle my finger hoping someone would notice and talk to me. I wanted to write my message to tell everyone, 'I'm still here. Inside me is Airlie. I have so much to say.'

Over six long but life-sustaining years, these daily rituals went on as I lived at Julia Farr: I could just describe them as feeding, dressing and watering me, with minimal therapy. I would think of all the good times I'd had before my accident: of my trips overseas with my parents, and also on my own to England and Japan. I would imagine I was in England, visiting my favourite places, or in Japan, brushing up my Japanese language skills, so I could teach my students Japanese better. The seasons came and went. I made some progress. I was shifted to different wards, met new faces, new routines. I would take time to readjust, but I was unable to assert myself or respond. I was bound by ritual, routine, habit, culture.

I had several operations to correct my tightened limbs, limbs which were now unresponsive. I could not go home until I had made a good recovery. I had to concentrate on the things I could do – my strengths. This was a state of mind I realised and one I must nurture. I set my sights on being able to communicate. Couldn't I do that? I had been an articulate person, once. I could be that again.'

4

A Miracle

About five years after my accident, my right arm recovered some movement after my operations. A miracle occurred; it started with a 'sign'. One day, Mum noticed me trying to move my fingers in a strange new way. In an effort to help me, she put a pen in my hand and supported my wrist. Mum asked me to try to write. I tried, but immediately the pen dropped out of my hand. After several attempts, I wrote some squiggles.

At Mum's request, the occupational therapist was asked to see if she could help me learn to write again. She made me a special penholder and glove so I wouldn't drop the pen, and I learnt to write again. My first word I wrote was my name, 'Airlie'. Then I answered a question from the therapist when she asked me if I wanted to learn to write again. I wrote, 'Yes. I need your help', my first clear message for six years!

In a letter to friends, 7 June 1997, Mum wrote to tell them of my progress.

> Dear (Friends),
>
> 'You are the God who performs miracles' (Psalm 77:14).
>
> At the end of March 1997, Airlie began to write. We had been aiming for this goal for some months, since November 1996, but she had really only started to learn to hold the pen and draw a straight line by the end of February. At the beginning of March she changed to a new occupational therapist, and after a few weeks of Airlie working with her, we went in to Julia Farr one day (26 March 1997) to find the place was buzzing with excitement. We discovered that Airlie had not only written

her name, but had communicated that she wanted to write and 'said' (wrote) to the occupational therapist (OT), 'I need your help'.

I must admit we were amazed and somewhat of a doubting Thomas until we saw it happen. A few days after, we went away for a decent holiday, our first long break since Airlie's accident. We were away three and a half weeks. When we returned, we discovered Airlie was writing perfect sentences with correct spelling and grammar. On 10 April 1997, Airlie wrote,

The progress in such a short time was incredible. The OT taught us how to support Airlie's elbow to help her steady her arm. She wears a special splint to hold her pen so it does not slip from her fingers. When we found we could get her to write, we believed it was true.

Neti writing with Airlie, 1997.

Some of her early favourite sayings were –
'Mum is my manager.
Dad is my very best friend.
My sister is my good mate.
I have a whole new world opening.
My writing is worth recording, mostly.'

Some comments were succinct and to the point, even if not favourable!

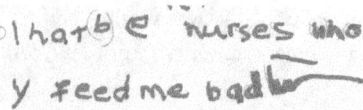

She also used the word 'masterful' and 'master' many times. There was a message here – being in control of herself was paramount.

She has galloped since then. Her progress to date is writing letters to all her friends. She writes (prints) about six sentences at a time, and as her writing is rather large (using a texta), she fills up a lot of pages quickly. She is now anxious to write in cursive and that is something she is working on improving. She wants other people to learn to help her write too, so, as she wrote, 'A whole new world is opening up to me.'

We have discovered in the course of all this that her memory, cognition, thinking ability, even mathematical ability is still intact. She can make decisions, and wry comments about the situation. Her sense of humour is terrific. She remembers all about her music and what she used to do. We have come to the conclusion that she has been 'locked in' all this time, and by God's miracle her brain has unlocked the part to allow her to communicate.

The rewards for Airlie are immense. She can now give her parents orders, and express exactly what she wants, what she likes and dislikes. We have a much better way of meeting her needs.

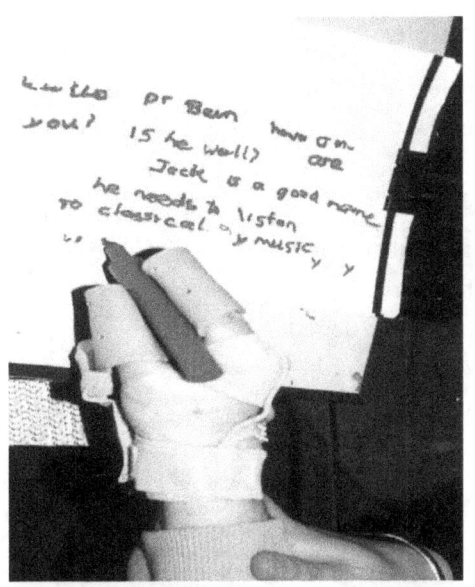

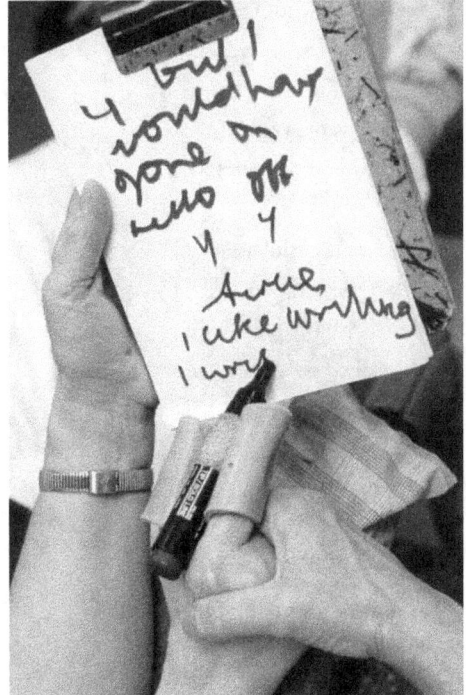

Airlie's writing showing penholder.

My operations

My arms tightened up a lot, so I had to have them straightened. I had several operations at private hospitals. I was swathed in bandages and I had a big cushion under my right arm to stretch it out. But I was happy my arm was better. I was not in those hospitals very long, but it was a pleasant escape from Julia Farr.

I had five visits to hospital for surgery. I was in pain a lot, but now I can write, so it was worth it.

Bent Arms

Arms contracted,
elbows bent,
fingers, wrists,
all curled the wrong way.
My brain was sending messages –
'Curl your arms,' it said.
I didn't want to,
but my arms obeyed.
I couldn't bend or stretch,
or write,
or make a masterful attempt
to pick something up.
My arms give me great pain,
trouble, distress.
I was the most plastered person
alive.
I lost count of those plasters.
Was it fifty or sixty
or seventy-five?
I was always covered in plaster
somewhere.
One day the decision was made.
Straighten those limbs.

Make them functional.
So begins a series of operations.
'Oh God,' I prayed,
'make my arms straight.'
I had great faith in my surgeons.
They were miraculous
in their achievements.
They cut and stitched,
corrected and plastered.
Three big operations transformed
my bent limbs.

I was not without pain.
I had an almighty endurance test,
but we won,
my surgeons and I.
Now I can write.
Admittedly I need support,
but I can communicate
after five long years of silence.
My arms are no longer painful.
I can be dressed more easily.
I am learning to hold a rod.
And I am writing a book
to tell you all about
my great progress.
My masterful right hand
functions again.

5 July 1998

I wrote this poem for my orthopaedic specialist, Dr Greg Bain, who encouraged me in my writing after I was recovering from surgery he had performed.

5
Letters from Prison

Many friends offered support to Mum and Dad by coming to read to me, both at Julia Farr and at home. I looked forward to those times, as I love reading. One of those kind friends was Margaret Dickson, from our church, who has read to me for over twenty-four years now.

The article on the following two pages was written by Margaret for *Trinity Times* in September 1997. Margaret and I taught in Sunday school together at Holy Trinity.

Barbara Kingsmill, mentioned in the article, also became a very dear friend to me and I loved her reading and singing choruses to me. Sadly she became very ill. I wrote poems for her to encourage her as she faced death. Here is one poem.

Ode to Barbara

Great is His faithfulness,
Lord on high,
almighty, powerful.
We trust in Him day by day.
Do not look back,
look up, not down.
Depend on Him for strength,
don't wear a frown.
We uphold you in prayer,
rely on His Spirit.
We will be together
with God forever.
We will read again, soon.

LETTERS FROM PRISON

Imagine spending five and a half years in prison, not being able to speak to anyone. That's what life must have been like for Airlie Kirkham since her accident in September, 1991, unable to speak or walk or do anything for herself. What was going on in her mind all that time, when she could not communicate in the usual ways with those around her?

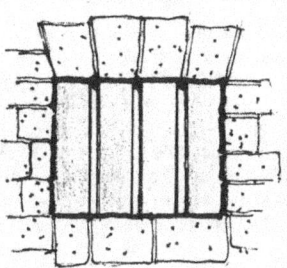

Now we are beginning to find out, for one day last March, with the Occupational Therapist (OT) supporting her wrist and elbow, Airlie began to write, with a felt-nibbed pen held in position by thermo-plastic splints. First of all it was lines, left to right, which she had been able to do before that day, then right to left, following the OT's instructions, then going down onto the next line without lifting the pen. Then Netti, the OT asked her to draw vertical lines, up and down, and then a circle, which came out rather wobbly, but still the circle was completed. Netti then asked her to write several other letters, which were all completely legible, and then she wrote her name. AIRLIE.

Netti asked her several questions, to which Airlie wrote Y or N, and finally Netti asked Airlie if there was something she wanted to say. **She wrote, slowly and carefully**: "I need help". "This is goose-bump stuff", whispered Netti. Since that exciting moment she has been writing with great confidence, perfect spelling, punctuation and grammar, saying all the things she must have wanted to say for years, and which we have longed to know. Here are some samples: "I like listening to ABC FM.

Others who helped me at this time were Nancy Webb and Amy Ramsay. Both were my former teachers at Woodlands, and I am indebted to their loving care and prayers for me ten years after I left school.

Nancy was my deputy headmistress and a mathematics teacher. She came to Julia Farr once a week to help Mum and Dad with my exercises, and this despite her own limitations with one arm lame from

Please leave my radio on ABC FM." "I like my food more tasty. Please use more pepper and salt, and tomato sauce on everything. But not on my desserts!" "My wish is to go to church every week so I can thank God for helping me to be able to write". As her mother said to me some years ago, her personality is still the same, and so is her sense of humour.

When I began reading to her, I didn't know what to choose, and read some of Kipling's Just So stories, including "How the Elephant got its Trunk", great literature not for children only, and some lovely Scottish folk tales. Gradually I realised that, if she was still the same very intelligent Airlie, I should be reading really adult stories, and found that she seemed to respond more to Christian biography and autobiography, because she would raise her head, turn and look at me straight in the eye, and sometimes smile at me. They were great moments. I also began reading more of the Bible, a chapter at a time, rather than little snippets, which I hoped were comforting, and, all the time, poetry of all kinds, from Chaucer to modern. I gained an insight into her tastes because she had once written in a loose-leaf folder, all her favourite poems.

Barbara Kingsmill has come to the same conclusions as I have, and has been reading C S Lewis, not only the Narnia series but also, the adult books, which are very challenging. Barbara finds too that Airlie responds to her singing, turns her head towards her, smiles, and her face lights up as she almost chuckles. One day I became convinced that she understood everything that was said when I told her that I would put some more lanolin on her lips. I turned away to pick up the tube and turned back to her to find her lips pursed, waiting for me to put the ointment on them. So the little signs were there, perhaps only to be seen once.

Now there is much excitement and joy as each week she writes more. "My memory is improving now that I am writing", and "My hand is becoming more masterful". She remembers people and things she has been told, and now wants to be able to read for herself, to achieve more and to be "warden of myself". **With her courage and determination and her faith in God, I am sure she will continue to surprise us.**

MARGARET DICKSON

polio as a child. Freda Dingwall, a teacher colleague of Mum's from Henley High School days, also came to read to me regularly after she retired from school, and she still continues to this day, reading to me my favourite classical novels.

Amy taught Religious Education at Woodlands for many years. She attended St Richard's Anglican Church Lockleys, and in the prayer circle which she convened at the church monthly, she found a place for me. She reported on my progress over the years, and encouraged members to pray for me at each meeting.

This was not the only church sustaining me with prayer besides my own, Holy Trinity. My slow but steady progress showed how effective sincere prayer can be. St Michael's Church Mitcham was another faithful church who also prayed for me in their Prayer Circle. Our good friend Audrey Fuhrer is a member of this community who faithfully visited me in Julia Farr and now at home regularly to help with my exercises. There were many other churches and persons unknown to me who prayed for me through these difficult times.

I was moved to a single room in specialised care. This greatly assisted my eating skills and removed distractions to my physical therapy and recreational therapy programs. My daily program was full of stimulating activities involving many carers and friends coming for exercising, reading, Bible reading and other activities, all with the main goal of providing me with stimulation. As I lacked movement, I needed constant change of position to control my increased muscle tone. I benefited greatly from the relaxed environment of the single room.

Airlie in her JFS specialised care room.

6
Awakenings

I mentioned in chapter four that Neti had helped me learn to write again. This was defining moment in my new life, and this moment led to further discoveries.

It was now known that parts of my brain were still intact, in spite of my accident. I still loved good music, and I still had a sense of humour. Now I could express all this in words.

At first I wrote in printing like a kindergarten child, and then as I grew more passionate about my success, I literally ran into cursive writing. It took me over six months to learn writing again and I have not stopped since. The pen and its holder are my lifeline to the world around me. I need help to steady my arm, but I can write.

I knew I could still think from the time of my accident, but only Mum and Dad knew of my dilemma. I wrote all sorts of things. I proved I was not vegetative but locked in. Now I was free at last. My first feelings were that I had the whole world opening up in front of me. I wrote down all my questions. I had so much to catch up. I felt wonderful, as I could talk to Mum and tell her all my problems and feelings. It was like a door opening, and all my thoughts came pouring out. I felt so excited now I could talk to everyone.

Since that exciting movement, I have been writing with great confidence, perfect spelling, punctuation and grammar, saying what I have wanted to say for years. I was always a good speller and I still am.

I told my carers in JFS, 'I like listening to ABC FM and I like my food more tasty. Please use more pepper and salt and tomato sauce on everything! But not on my desserts!'

I felt so happy that I could tell everyone that my brain could still think,

> I want tomato sauce on most things but not on my dessarts, my many other ~~new~~ mornays and weetbix.

that I wasn't stupid or unable to understand, because some people treated me that way. Even today, people still often say to Mum, 'Can she understand what I'm saying?' I felt so much love in my heart to God, who had answered the prayers to survive and to help me communicate again, for my family who had looked after me so well. I was excited, as I knew I could get back control in my life again.

I turned to poetry. Poetry has always inspired me. It moves my soul; it conjures up feelings and moods. My ideas became reality. I wrote poetry about my dreams to come home. With Mum guiding my hand, I composed poems of thanks and praise to God, and wrote on many other subjects. In time, the number of poems grew to over two hundred. I will share two of these poems with you. They were also published in the *Adelaide Advertiser* on Saturday 29 January 2000.

Power in Myself

Imagine not being in control
of yourself.
Not able to speak,
nor communicate your desires.
My situation was exactly that.
I was locked in myself,
I could not decide anything.
I was powerless,
a grown adult who
had to rely on my parents
for everything.
Power in oneself is masterful,

but I wasn't the master.
I wanted to be in control;
my head injury prevented it.
I was always frustrated,
not able to make my own decisions,
my own choices.
My own wishes were
never possible
while I couldn't communicate.
My wish was to be able to talk.
Power eluded me.
Mastery of communication was lost.
A lost soul who,
above all else,
wanted to thrive on speech,
on relationships with others.
My wish was not granted
for nearly six long years.

2 November 1998

What Love Means

Love is unlimited in my home.
We all love one another.
with infinitesimal depth.
Love is not masterful
unless it is coupled with a family
who are one with each other.
Members of my family,
are loving and kind.
They thrive on love.
Love which knows no bounds,
is a mode for anyone

who is loving.
We are loving when we know God.
Love is from Him.
It abides for ever.
We must make the best of a situation.
Love holds us together
like a chain mesh in a jewellery piece.
Love is timeless, like the universe
showing all its majesty.
We thrive on love in our family.
We achieve all things through our love
interwoven in all we do and say.
We are masterful always in our family love.
My wish was to come home.
Love is unlimited in my home.
My wish was not granted
for nearly six long years.

Airlie in the Advertiser, Saturday, 29 January 2000. (Photo by Leon Mead)

Throughout the time of my rehabilitation and recovery, I never felt like giving up. I have a strong faith in God and He has sustained me. I have trusted Him to provide me with all my needs. I want to tell the world that miracles still happen and God works them in His own time. To other families with relatives in a similar situation, I would say, never give up hope: be strong and determined. These qualities will help them through the difficult times. They need to communicate to their loved one because even people in a coma can hear and think. They are sensitive to their environment and need to be aware of their family's strong hope and faith in them.

I wanted to tell my family that I would be forever grateful to them for standing by me in such a tragic situation. They have suffered as much as me in a different way, but they are strong too and have great faith in God, which has encouraged and supported me. My faith has never wavered during all this time. In fact, it is stronger because of the many blessings we have all received.

After learning to write in 1997, I started communicating and writing poetry. By 2016, I had written over four hundred poems and I am putting all my thoughts and feelings into this story about my recovery.

Looking From My Window At Julia Farr

The view from my room
is wonderful.
I follow the seasons.
The trees change colours
and fall.
They regrow and start
the cycle again.

Autumn is my favourite view,
the mellow colours
of a splendid liquidambar.
Liquid gold,
a name with a better effect
would be more appropriate.
Rustic hues,
reds, browns,
gold and yellow.
The lorikeets come every year,
to savour the tasty seeds
in the catkins.
I counted twenty eight one day.

Their colourful plumage,
blended with the liquid gold.
They gave me great joy,
as I watched from my window.
Too soon the winter winds stripped the tree
of its finery, bleak and bare.
Now I could see afar
to the crisp cold city,
to the hub of life
of busy people.
But it was not impressive,
mellowness turned to coldness;
next came the vibrancy of spring.
My view was changing,
to the soft greens of spring,
of new life.
I thought of my new life
which I hope would begin soon,
at home.
Flowers adorned the gardens.
The roses brightened my view.

Summer was hot.
We drew the shades
in my room with a view.
But I didn't mind;
soon that would pass
and it would return to show me
my kaleidoscope of autumn colours.
My own room which I enjoyed.

The following poem was written for my resident doctor at the time, Dr Susan Hooper, in recognition of all the blood tests she tried to take from me.

Blood Tests

Blood, veins,
needles, bottles,
readings for all things.
No veins, despair,
nurses flinch,
doctors, squibs,
call IMVS.
We're here now.
Drop all.
Collecting blood,
it's a breeze.
Not more tests!
I've just had some.
They perform
like Dracula.
Why do they want so much?
Tests are good,
nil problems.

Next week,
they'll be back.
We love Airlie's blood.
We must collect
more and more,
to see if the readings are fine.
Now I'm home,
blood is clear,
I'm out of their clutches.
Who is their next victim?
It's not me!

9 August 1998

I mentioned earlier how reading Dr Ted Freeman's book had been useful in the early days after my accident. After we had read his book, Mum contacted him. He lived in Sydney and he advised us to contact Dr Roger Rees of Flinders University who, he assured us, would be very helpful in our situation. Roger became a great friend, adviser and encourager to us over many years. He was a friend and colleague of Ted's and together they provided much advice and support.

It was Roger who introduced us to Ted in person. Dr Freeman was a well-known and respected specialist in brain injury. He was connected with Mead Hospital in Sydney, Director of the Research Division of the Australian Brain Foundation. He has written many papers on coma arousal, coma arousal intervention and the locked-in syndrome, as well as his book. He had served some time in Vanuatu as a medical missionary, and was Director in Vanuatu (New Hebrides) and Superintendent of the Rehabilitation Hospital.

On one occasion, Roger brought Ted to Adelaide for lectures at Flinders University and private consultations with persons with ABI.

The day Ted arrived in Adelaide, I was home for a long weekend. Roger brought him to our home straight from the airport, which is only a five-minute drive away. 'I want you to meet a young lady who had a motor vehicle accident and sustained an ABI,' he said. 'She is remarkable in that she appears to be aware, but she is unable to communicate.'

After observing me and talking to my parents for some time, Ted explained that he was confident that I was aware and perceptive of all that was going on around me, but that I was locked in. Ted described this as not being vegetative, as many had assumed, but being unable to communicate my thoughts and feelings in any way. Ted told us how we are all sensitive to the environment around us, and improvements would depend on that.

At last, I thought. Someone believes I am still here. I am still Airlie who has an active brain cognitively. I just can't use my muscles which control speech and movement. I was more eager than ever to escape the confines of JFS and come home to my old favourite environment.

Roger presented a program called 'What is the Locked-in State?', broadcast on *Ockham's Razor* on Radio National in August 1997. He said,

> From an economic rationalist's view of rehabilitation or a simplistic absolute view that a person is either cured or not cured, people in the locked-in state are considered of no account. There is a young woman in a local hospital who uses a large felt-tipped pen to write notes and letters about the poetry of Eliot and Whitman, and the prose of Jane Austen, or record her feelings about the music of Mozart. She has been in the locked-in state for six years, swaddled like a newborn, unable to speak or move unaided, often experiencing a total lapse into infancy. Yet in those six years, her mind has remained intact, eager to emerge when the appropriate appointments arrived. Her parents have maintained a six-year vigil, believing that an intact person still existed in their daughter's paralysed body. She still cannot speak but her writings now invoke the supremacy of her inner senses of memory, dreams, reasoning and imaginings. There is now a curious reversal of views by those who believed that her brain damage was total and global. Her parents are surely vindicated, as their daughter's meticulous writings spread before our eyes can provide evidence of the mystery of human resilience and of the duality of the interaction of the brain and mind.
>
> Jean-Dominique Bauby a forty-two-year-old father of two, and editor-in-chief of *Elle* magazine in Paris, suffered a massive stroke which left him speechless but able to move only one muscle, in his eyelid. His mind remained active and alert. By signalling with his eyelid, he 'dictated' *The Diving Bell and the Butterfly*, blinking to indicate each letter. Bauby's writings and the young woman's letters about her intact memory of poetry and prose, as well as her memory of and ability to respond to Japanese, must reawaken interest in the persistent problem of how to recognise, utilise and facilitate the skills and talents that reside in the 'locked-in'.

About this time, it was decided I could learn to use a Delta Talker machine to communicate my wishes. I spent much time learning how it worked. It was like a computer keyboard, with icons representing words and phrases. I had to scan through them using a switch, so I memorised the icons and practised in earnest. I set about raising the money to purchase such a costly machine. Sometime later, The *Advertiser* for Saturday 29 January 2000 presented an article about my situation. It included the two poems above and my desire to have a Delta Talker talking machine to help me communicate.

On 11 February 2000, in an uplifting twist of fate, Immanuel College, Novar Gardens, read the *Advertiser* article and decided to raise money for my Delta Talker fund. The college's coordinator, Ivan Christian, said the school's Kavel House would donate money raised from sale of student portraits to help me. They were moved by the incredible story of my strength and faith in a powerless situation. The fund-raiser was a small part of the school's involvements in community life. I was so grateful. The students came to my house to give me a cheque and it was a delightful occasion for all of us.

7
Hopes and Aspirations

Home – at last!

I had been longing to go home for some time. My thoughts and feelings for my own home while at Julia Farr are explicitly described in the following poem which I wrote before I left the institution.

Julia Farr

Imagine living
in a big institution,
with hundreds of people,
rooms and wards.
What will it feel like,
with no privacy,
no where to be alone,
no one to talk to?
Will it be friendly,
or will it be impersonal,
uncaring,
unable to be masterful
in all it does?
Or will it be a home
for all those who reside there?
I have been a resident
for six long years;
imagine my feelings,
my despair,

in not being in my home.
Will I ever get out of this place?
My hope tells me I will,
soon.
I will leave behind
memories.
Of how I hated being there,
memories,
of the nurses who looked after me,
memories,
of the therapists
who helped me recover.
Now I will see Julia Farr
from a distance,
from a way off.
I will think sometimes
of my friends
I have left behind.
I will not miss Julia Farr.
It will become a dream.

At last it became a reality in March 1998. Carers were organised, a new room and bathroom had been built over the previous twelve months and equipment brought in. I arrived home in great excitement.

Coming Home

I am home at last.
I am able to have my own space,
my own room,
my own time
to do as I wish.
I am making my own decisions,
my own other things.

I am choosing my own clothes,
my own food,
my own radio and TV programs.
I am enjoying sitting by the window
overlooking our garden.
I can hear the birds
singing in the trees.
We had a picnic under the patio.
The Abbey Girls came.
We talked books.
I was so happy.
We had a welcome home cake.
I was home for good.
Welcoming me was
my newly painted room.
We had boxes everywhere,
clothes and furniture,
but I was home.
Home sweet home.
Oh how the word 'home'
brings tears to my eyes.
My vision,
my dream
my longing,
have come to fruition,
at last.
I want to thank Mum and Dad
for helping me achieve my goal,
and God, for supporting us all.

I have been living at home since March 1998. I have been able to write for many years now, and I am delighted to share my thoughts, memories and reflections with you. My strength has come from God, whose steadfast love for me never fails.

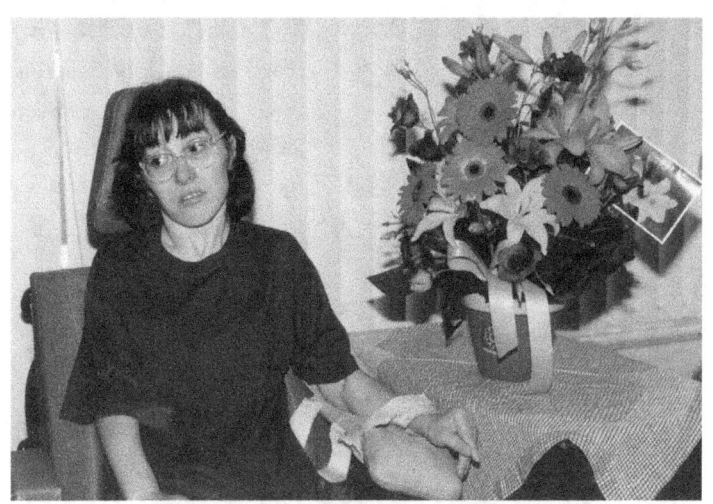
Airlie's first day at home.

(Photo: Classic Natural Images, SA)

After I came home, my sister Katrina and Dale Rycroft were married on 11 April. The house was in a flutter – painters, presents, people. I don't know how we managed it all, as everything was new to us all. But it was a wonderful wedding at Holy Trinity Church, Adelaide, the pioneer church of South Australia.

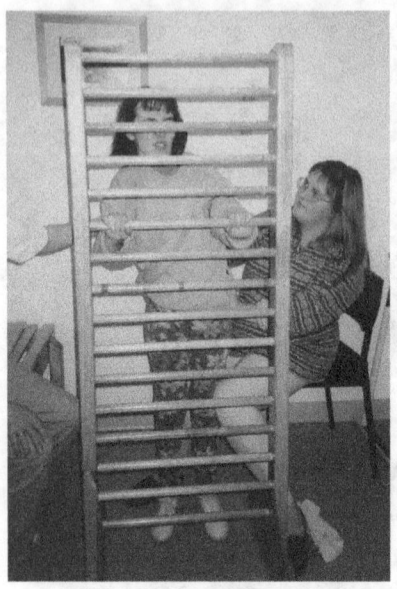

Airlie and carer at Springboard.

I undertook another rehabilitation course lasting three years. It was called Springboard and was run by the Brain Injury Network of SA (BINSA). It consisted of a program of exercises, speech therapy, conductive education and social activities. I enjoyed this two days a week.

In June 2001, I was asked by the ABC producer Michael O'Donnell to debate the question whether doctors should have the right to turn off life support to those who are severely injured like I was. The debate was shown on ABC TV's *Catalyst*.

The question I was asked to discuss during the program was 'What was it like when you were locked in?'

This was my reply:

> I felt locked in because I couldn't write or speak. I could see everything and everyone. I knew who they were. I could hear people talking to me, about me, and saying things I didn't like. I wasn't asked if I wanted to do something. I would have liked people to talk to me properly, as I could hear and understand…I could smell OK… I felt very frustrated, at times angry, because no one would come near me [at times] or talk to me, only Mum and Dad, my visitors, or the therapists.
>
> I couldn't tell people what I wanted. I was frustrated because I wasn't in control of myself. I used to wriggle my fingers hoping someone would notice. I wanted to write my message to tell everyone I'm still here.
>
> Inside me is Airlie. I have so much to say.
>
> After I could communicate, it felt wonderful, as I could talk to Mum and tell her all my problems and feelings. It was like a door

opening, and all my thoughts came pouring out. I felt free at last. I was so excited now I could talk to everyone.

I felt so happy that I could tell everyone that my brain could still think, that I wasn't stupid or unable to understand, because some people treated me that way. I felt excited because I knew I could get back some control in my life. In my heart, I felt so much love for my family, who had looked after me so well. I wanted to tell then I loved them and that I wanted to go home to live, but I wanted to write better before I did. I hated being in an institution, but there was no money to ensure I could be looked after at home. That came later.

I want to tell the world that miracles still happen and God works them in His own time. I would tell the world to trust in God and to always have hope and belief that a miracle will happen. I want to tell families never to give up hope, to be strong and determined...

During that year (1998) several magazines contacted us to do a feature story about my 'awakening' or becoming 'unlocked'. Journalist Kate Cole-Adams wrote a story about me which was featured in the Melbourne *Age* and the *Sydney Morning Herald* on Saturday 19 December 1998. In Kate's words, 'Cases of severe brain injury are often thought to be hopeless. Coma is considered living death. But

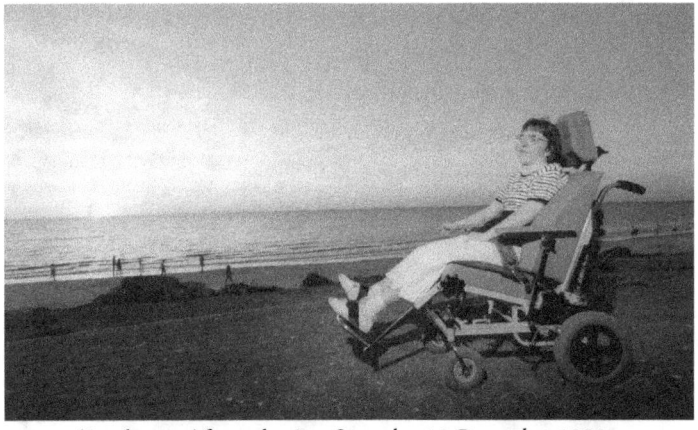

'Awakenings' from the Age, Saturday 19 December 1998 – Sunset at Henley Beach. (Photo by Bryan Charlton)

how often are alert minds trapped inside unresponsive bodies?' It described how important communication was to people like me who cannot walk and talk.

The *Women's Weekly* article, May 2000, featured a story 'Local girl back from the brink'. This was connected with a feature they were running about real-life awakenings. Basically the story by Caroline Chisholm was very similar to that of *The Age*; it also described my need for a talking machine to help me communicate.

In December 2002, my three years in Springboard ended, and I decided to take on some other interests. I joined the Passion of Poets group, which meets monthly to read and work on poems members of the group have recently written.

To Poetry, My Love

Words I read from Isaiah
stimulate my thoughts –
'Let me sing for my beloved
a love song'
Isaiah, a master of vocabulary.
How is it that poetic thoughts
from words from so long ago,
reach out to me –
prophetic, encouraging,
wise and thought-provoking?
Down the ages
poetry has soothed mankind,
kept him strong, emotional
compassionate.
Medieval Chaucer pens romance,
earthy and miraculous tales;
Shakespeare indites history,
proverbial sayings,
well-spoken quotations.

Coleridge bestows a meditative mind,
Wordsworth calls up memories,
sensuous nostalgia,
emotions recollected in tranquillity,
warming hues and seasons of happiness.
Keats finds melancholy in delight,
a dream world.
Pushkin strides there;
shows a free mind,
lyrical, satirical, intuitive and realist,
revealing the depth of his soul in poetry.
Wilfred Owen evokes
the depth and pity of war.
Auden, with unsentimental
but thoughtful imagery,
is a poet of his time.
Modern poetry expresses
deep feeling, desires, whims, fancies.
The words of Isaiah ring again in my mind:
'Be glad and rejoice
for ever in that which I create.'
I turn to poetry at any time.
It calms my being,
an escape to new worlds, new horizons.
Poetry stirs my soul.
I care only for my love,
my language of motivation and spirit,
my song of joy,
my love song.

                                                    June 2011

I was already a member of The Abbey Girls Book Club, where we read and discuss books by Elsie J. Oxenham. Set in England in the period 1900–1950, these books feature a school associated with an old English abbey. Traditional customs like May Day and May Queens are woven around the exciting adventures of the owner of the abbey, Joan, and all her school friends as they grow up to have their own families. Most years, we choose a queen of the club. I am Queen Daffodil and I was crowned while I was still in Julia Farr.

I became a member of the International Bible Study Fellowship in 2002. We have a weekly meeting to read and study the Bible. Each week I study a passage and answer the questions in my writing. I love doing this, but become quite upset if I miss out writing them for whatever reason. I have been able to attend church more often now that I am home.

But most of all, I wanted to take up the challenge of returning to Adelaide University. In 2002, I enrolled in a refresher subject from the Bachelor of Music, and with the support of my carer and mother I was able to achieve a distinction as the final result.

This encouraged me, and in 2003 I enrolled part-time for BMus

Airlie with her parents at church one Sunday at Holy Trinity Anglican, North Terrace, Adelaide. (Photo by Jill Phillips)

Honours Musicology and completed the first year with good results. I still need total support for daily activities, I still cannot walk and talk, but I can think and communicate using my pen and a Delta Talker machine which speaks for me. I feel lucky that I have been able to return to university and it is the best thing in my life at present. What the future holds I do not know. Writing tires me so I can only do a small amount at a time. However, writing would make me happy as a career, now that I can no longer teach. The path of life that I tread now is not the path I would have chosen myself. But I will walk it, with the strength of God, whose steadfast love has never failed me.

8
Thoughts and Feelings

Words are my lifeblood. I was very frustrated because I wanted to convey my message to everyone. Many people did not know what I wanted to do or say. I used to wriggle my fingers hoping someone would notice and talk to me. Since I learnt to write, a whole new world has opened up for me, as now I can communicate my thoughts and feelings in writing, in poetry, short stories and articles.

I wrote the paragraph below to Mum after she asked me about my thoughts and feelings.

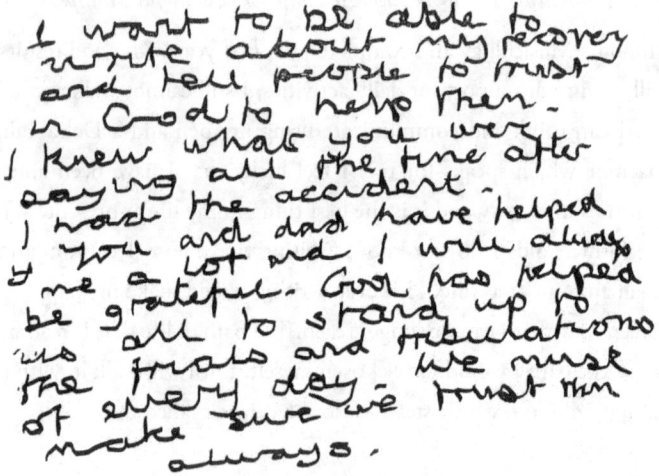

I wrote,

I want to be able to write about my recovery and tell people to trust in God to help them. I knew what you [that is, Mum and Dad] were saying all the time after I had the accident. You and

Dad have helped me a lot and I will always be grateful. God has helped us all to stand up to the trials and tribulations of every day. We must make sure we trust Him always.

Take His powerful words into your heart and believe them.

Words are my Lifeblood

> We take for granted good speech.
> Articulate though we may be,
> we are not able to communicate,
> unless our vocal chords will respond.
> Words give us a mastery of ourselves,
> which, when we have lost them,
> make us more reliant on others.
> We rely on the grace of God
> for the gift of speech.
> He nurtures us from infancy as we attempt to speak.
> When we are grown,
> we think we are able to control
> the world with words,
> But we cannot.
> We are speechless
> when we have a head injury.
> I am ever thankful
> for the gift of words;
> a gift so precious,
> one I wish to share with everyone.
> A lifeblood to my whole being.

Now that I can write, there is no problem communicating with me. I have persisted with my writing until I can write quite quickly now. I love to talk with my pen and have my say. I have excellent hearing and can respond.

In 1997, I decided to seek my independence and wrote a letter to

Dear Sir,
I would like to have my Administration order cancelled.
I am able to communicate through my writing and I want to be able to manage my own affairs. My aim is to be independent. I am supported in this decision by my parents, my doctor and my social worker. They have written letters of support.
I hope that you will grant my request, as I do not need this order anymore now that I can communicate my wishes.
Yours faithfully
Airlie J. Kirkham
11th Nov. 97

the Guardianship Board who had managed my affairs up till now. This request was subsequently granted.

I also made good friends with Robyn Hester, former Chaplain at Memorial Hospital, who visited me several times while I was in Memorial Hospital and at home afterwards. The following letter from her was written for her Parish newsletter June 2000, Our Lady of the Sacred Heart Parish, Henley and Grange.

Robyn wrote,

> I first met Airlie Kirkham when I was doing chaplaincy work at Memorial Hospital in 1999. I had actually taught Latin with her mother Pam at Henley High School many years ago, but our ways had gone separately since then. I had not heard of her beautiful talented daughter Airlie's tragic accident eight years ago. Airlie's story has been told recently in the *Advertiser*, the *Women's Weekly* and on TV (*Catalyst* program). It is an inspiring story of a courageous faith-filled young woman, climbing a huge mountain, an image used by the Professor of Medicine on a TV program. He also acknowledged how essential for the climber is the support team, in this case, Airlie's loving family. With all that, Airlie has lost one thing she longs for passionately, the gift of speech.

9
Support from Others

Friends from my schooldays at Woodlands who were musicians with the Adelaide Symphony Orchestra decided to help me. In 2000 they organised a music concert to raise funds to help purchase a Delta Talker talking machine for me. I love music, and of course I have a music degree, so this seemed a fitting way to demonstrate my love of music.

Ode to Music

Music stirs my soul,
uplifts a mournful mood,
expresses feelings
of the innermost being;
compassion, thought,
the rhythm of life.
Music leads me
down life's path,
roads full of meaning,
people, places.
Music interprets a person's soul;
moods, desires created by a
life in all its modes.
Music inspires,
soothes ruffled spirits,
a frayed temper mellowed.
My heart rejoices.
Music brightens the day.

When I hear Bach,
I feel enlightened.
Mozart gives me feelings
of refinement.
Beethoven stirs the emotions within me.
Mahler makes me passionate and strong.
Elgar arouses my feelings of England,
of my heritage,
of my great love of this fine land.
Britten, my favourite composer of modern times.
brings great lyrical beauty to music.
Diversities of harmonies
enrich my soul.
Music makes me happy.
Praise God with music.
Sing songs in exaltation.
Most of all, thank God
for His gift to us.
Music will live within me forever.

7 May 2000

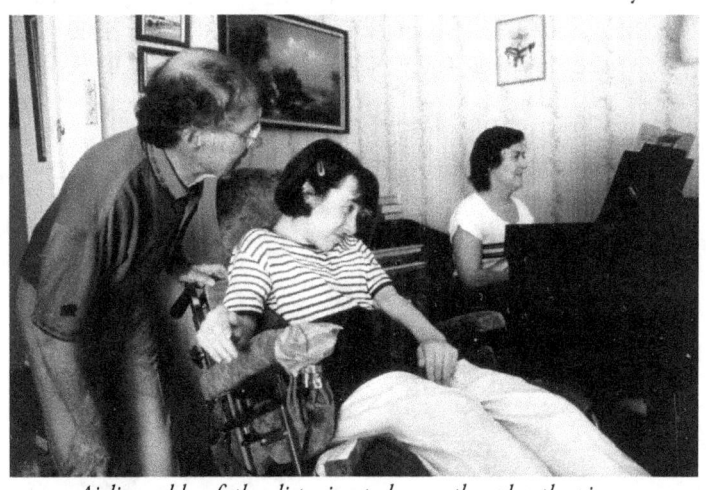

Airlie and her father listening to her mother play the piano.
(Photo courtesy of ABC TV Catalyst, Coma, Part 3, 20 September 2001)

An afternoon with Airlie

After a concert held at St Columba's Anglican Church, Hawthorn, on Sunday 21 May 2000, I wrote,

> The programme opened with Mozart's popular oboe quartet with strings. Paul Miller (oboe) showed a brilliant technique in the opening movement. The leader, Margaret Blades, led the group with verve. The second movement was sensitive and emotional, displaying the oboe's fine command of the lower register. The finale, in the form of a rondeau, deserved the strong applause.
>
> In between musical items, Meg Skuce read excerpts from my anthology of poetry. These outstanding readings added a spiritual and emotional dimension to the afternoon.
>
> Vivaldi's contribution, written when he was master in charge of music at a girl's school in Venice, was the splendid concerto for four violins played by four Woodlands old scholars who are also members of the Adelaide Symphony Orchestra. The Madrigal for violin and viola by Martinu was followed by two duets, Waltz in A major (Livtsky) and the Jamaican Rumba (Benjamin) arranged for two violins.
>
> The programme concluded with Bach's oboe and violin Concerto BWV 1060 in C minor, derived from a lost work often played by two claviers. The ensemble was magnificently directed by Margaret Blades, violin; with Paul Miller, oboe; Danielle Jacquillard, Julie and Jenny Newman, violin; Cecily Matthews, viola; and Alison Miller, cello.

The ambience of the church setting, together with the audience of supportive friends, made the afternoon most successful and inspirational.

In July 2000, another successful event was the Adelaide Rotary Club fund-raising concert for me, under the direction of Bruce Raymond.

Music Night

1st July 2000

Norwood Town Hall

featuring

Kensington & Norwood
Brass Band

Only $20 pp

Proceeds to help Airlie Kirkham's dream come true – to raise the funds for a Delta Talker

GET YOUR TICKETS TODAY

Contact: Bruce Raymond (W) 8416 6677
Fax: 8416 6753
Mobile: 0414 758 786

★ **Barry Ion** ★ **Stephen Rowe**
of the 5AA breakfast team

K & N Brass meets the stars

plus a number of other surprise performers

proceeds support a special project of the Rotary Club of Adelaide

---

Where to get Rotary on the Web
District 9500:
 http//www.users.on.net/krwil/d9500web/
Rotary International:
 http//www.rotary.org
Rotarians on the Internet:
 http//www.roti.org
Rotary Down Under:
 http//www.rotarnet.com.au

10
Helping Others

In 2002 I was asked to take part in the Choice presentation for Road Safety organised by SA Police. I visited many high schools and delivered my message on road safety by means of my Delta Talker machine.

This is what I had to say:

Hello everyone.

I'm Airlie Kirkham.

I am happy to be here to talk to you today, or perhaps I should say, my machine will talk to you. Well, that's funny, having a machine to talk to you, but you see, I lost my speech in my car accident.

I used to be fluent in languages. I was a Japanese, English and Music teacher ten years ago. I had a car accident which changed my life totally. I would like to tell you what happened.

I was twenty-five years old. I had a good job, and life, lots of friends, and a boyfriend. I lost control of my car on a dirt road near Balaklava. I was going to a friend's kitchen tea and had lost my way. When the accident happened, I was not speeding, nor being stupid, nor had I had alcohol. I was in the wrong place and I hadn't learnt how to drive on gravel roads in the country. I was just unfamiliar with the road conditions, and how to over-correct the steering when my car wheel caught the gravel. I shouldn't have been on a gravel road, but as I said I was lost.

I don't remember anything that happened, as I woke up in the Royal Adelaide Hospital after several weeks in a coma. They tell me I veered across the road and hit another car. As a result, I received a very severe head injury, resulting in permanent brain damage, and some broken bones. I was very critical. I was not expected to live. My parents were holidaying in Hong Kong at that time, and they had to return immediately to Adelaide. My whole family and friends were in great trauma. They sat by my bedside day and night for several months. I was unable to respond to anyone.

After two months in Royal Adelaide Hospital, I was moved to the Julia Farr Centre. There, I underwent rehabilitation, for six long years before I could go home. During that time I lost most of my friends, I lost my job, and I spent every day doing therapy. But I was only able to recover partially. Broken bones will mend, but brain damage won't. My arms contracted up, and my muscles wouldn't work. I still can't walk or talk, but I learnt again many things you take for granted: to sit up, to stand with support, to eat, to drink, to go to the toilet, and to communicate again. I didn't learn that for a long time. I had many operations to straighten my arms. I had very good occupational therapists who made me a special penholder and taught me to write again. I could communicate after six years of silence. Can you imagine what it is like not to be able to speak for six years? Now a whole new world opened up for me.

Because of my acquired brain injury, my life is totally changed. I live in a wheelchair. I am dependent on carers to dress and feed me. I can't even do my own hair. I stay at home a lot. It is not easy for me to get out. My friends rarely visit me. My parents spend their whole lives looking after me with the help of paid carers.

How would you like to be a grown adult still being looked after by your mother?

When I went to the country, I thought it was just the same as driving in the city. Now I realise that isn't true. I should have been better prepared, and more familiar with the route, and the road conditions.

My ABI means I get fatigued easily. I can't always eat or sleep properly. I can't go out to enjoy a meal. My muscle tone becomes very rigid at times and makes me very uncomfortable. I forget things occasionally too, and often no one talks to me. I can't enjoy many of the activities which I formerly did. I loved reading. Now I have to wait until someone can read to me.

This year I have returned to university. It is ten years after my accident. I'm trying to pick up my studies. I already have two degrees and a diploma, but I need something more to stimulate my mind. I can't do it now without support. I am unable to have a job, but I love writing. Maybe I can develop that into something. I am trying to write a book to tell others of my experiences. Writing is slow and tedious, and tires me out, so I can only write for about an hour at once.

Today, I would like to encourage every one of you to be very careful on the roads. Think through every plan you have when you go driving, and if it is unfamiliar territory, take care, find out information, and even take a special driving course if it involves driving in country areas.

Don't think it won't happen to you, because you never know. Be careful.

Don't throw away opportunities. Always think safety, not just for yourself, but for others too. Thank you for letting me share my experiences with you. If you would like to ask me any questions, I would be happy to answer them. Thank you for listening.

After one of my presentations at Walford Girls' School, I received a complimentary email in 2002 from the coordinator of the Choice program, Karen Jenkinson. She wrote,

Hi Airlie,

Just a quick note to say 'CONGRATULATIONS' on a job well done. You were a star yesterday.

Even Kym the policeman was overwhelmed by your presentation. Kym is never stuck for words (until yesterday) – in fact he often gets teased because he never shuts up.

Your message came across well. It has been well written. It has an impact with a strong and informative message. The Walford girls were very emotional after your presentation and I know they appreciated your willingness to be there to tell them your story.

Thanks Airlie and welcome aboard to the team of Choice presenters.

Karen.

Thursday, 26 September 2002

In 2004, a book by Michelle Hamer, *It couldn't happen to me... BUT IT DID*, was published by Lothian Press. Michelle came from

Melbourne to interview me and to write my story in mostly my words. I proved I was not vegetative but locked-in. She was pleased to add the story of my new form of communication to her book of similar stories from like persons in Australia.

In 2005, the death of Terry Schiavo, a forty-one-year-old American woman who lay in a Florida hospital, raised around the world many of the delicate issues of whether anyone has the right to decide when another human being should die – that is, should life support be turned off? *Woman's Day* looked at all sides of this emotionally charged debate and asked several Australian families their opinions. Mum and I discussed the issue with reporter Sarah Marinos, and a feature was published on 18 April 2005. This debate was controversial; I felt playing God was dangerous with unpredictable outcomes. 'I don't think you should ever give up hope,' I said.

In June 2005, the magazine *Marie Claire* ran a similar feature series entitled 'Life, Death Or Limbo'. If this happened to you, what would you want? It featured persistent vegetative persons around the world. Lisa Dabscheck examined and continued the debate with two Australian families. I illuminated the case for living. 'After the doctors said they didn't think I would survive, I set out to prove the doctors wrong,' I said. I was interviewed, and this article was written, at the time when my mother was tidying up my Bachelor of Music Honours thesis of 14,000 words, all of it written by me with my pen, in its beloved penholder.

When it was time for Lisa to leave, I motioned to Mum that I wanted to make a final comment, which I scribbled on my pad. 'I hope people will think it all through before they take the big step of switching it off. I wouldn't be here if they had switched it off.'

11
Life at Home

All through these years, I continued my daily routine of exercises, of work in my spa and on the plinth, my physio table. This has helped keep me in good physical shape and to reduce my muscle tone from becoming excessive. My carers help me with this and some of my long-standing friends. Also Margaret and Freda continue to come to read to me, as do the carers when they have a spare moment.

I love going for a 'walk' in the linear park near my home, as I don't go out very much. I write poems of happenings around my home and in the garden. I hope you enjoy this small selection.

Ducks

One duck came acalling
followed by his mate.
Together they graced our front door,
asking for breakfast – late!
We had no bread, not even a bun.
This was a problem to solve.
Then we remembered, hidden in fun,
some scones, discard we did resolve.
Because they were deep frozen,
leftovers from Nanna's batch,
we gave them a flip in the microwave,
and they were made to match.
The ducks were pleased and so were we,
the scones were old and tough.

They dispatched them with much glee,
for we'd had quite enough.
Breakfast over, they took to flight,
back to their native lea.
Will we see them again tonight?
We'll just have to wait and see.

28 November 2003

Cockatoos

Nuisances. Noises.
A flash of yellow or was it white?
They have landed.
Heads down, they scratch for food,
like dogs digging ditches,
insist on spoiling the turf.
What delicacy do they find?
Whoosh! They are off,
preferring to savour the scene
from above the branches,
perched on power lines,
thrusting their busy beaks into the air,
parading like tin soldiers along the wires,
dangerously surveying their damage.

Yellow crests call yellow crests.
Birds of a feather flock together;
in a flash they are off.
The call of the wild,
bird language is universal.
These birds are smart, educated.
Like pigs grubbing for truffles,
they have found another patch,
no concern of theirs whose soil they turn.

But they'll be back, in time,
hoping for a tasty meal
of bright yellow daffodil trumpets.
Will any bulbs bloom next spring?

March 2007

That Bird!

Black and white,
it plunges to earth
relentlessly, diving,
again and again.
A shadow in the window,
behind the blinds gaping
in the morning sun.
Is it a mirror image,
a likeness of itself
attracting a territorial drive?
Invisible in the murky green water
in the tank, hidden discreetly
from the outside eye,
a reptile, a turtle behaving like
a creature seeking company,
distracts its invader.
The slightest movement from within
and the bird is gone
as quickly as it came.
But it will return to try again. Soon.

September 2008

Morning Serenity

Autumn leaves framed on my computer,
an image of our front garden
in the small hours of dawn;
orange, brown, red and yellow,
reflect the early sun
as it vainly tries to warm a frosty morning.
The hue, unexpected, resplendent, vibrant,
reminds me of Keats' 'Ode to Autumn'.
It depicts the hour of morning serenity,
better than a landscape by Constable,
more defined than a Monet.
Into my room it brings the outside scene
unseen by me, tucked in my warm bed.
Though forgotten by early morning walkers,
those who are too brisk and busy
to notice its vivid beauty,
I have it whenever I desire,
in my own room, captured forever.
Outside it may never return
the way it was that morning.

18 November 2006

Rainy Afternoons

Sitting by my window
I can see the rain,
mellow in sound,
falling down.
I think of mists,
watery shallows
in the landscape.
Raging torrents

in the nearby river,
cause drains to froth,
full of pollution
swept along by the rain.
The hail comes suddenly,
the stones pelting down from
icy regions above, making
a din on the roof.
The grass is white
like a snowfall.
The storm stops
as quickly as it came.
All is still, the sky wan
and pale in a mysterious light.
It's like life; sudden changes,
unexpected happenings
sweep us along on the tide of time,
like that raging torrent.
All too soon it's over.
It happened and is gone.

October 2005

The Oak Tree

Standing tall, majestic,
traditional English, ornamental,
shut in by shadow from an overburdening canopy.
Now bare, denuded by winter winds,
divested of burnished acorns.
Needing a skilful manicure,
I wake each day to greet the tree.
The spring winds blow, drifting through the dead wood drear.
The sunlight shines on secret lots, darkness, and shade,

and finds a way through leafless limbs.
Season of changes.
There comes pruning, sawing, perhaps overwhelming,
dead boughs are gone.
The dawn slants through the recently cropped limbs.
In silence, the old tree pleads for new life, and,
reconciled to her losses, shoots forth in awakening leaf.
She sighs no more.
Like yellow shafts, slanting beams of morning sunlight
move warmly and discretely through the air.
The magic tree shakes away old leaves.
The yearly miracle unfolds. Buds rise and burst forth.
All is not lost.
Her beautiful rich green leaves open to the sun.
She brings forth flourishing fruits, golden flowers.
All the seasons take from her she will restore.
Now that she is rejuvenated, she stands proud,
keeping guard over my garden.
This is my oak.

September 2014

12
A Dream Come True

Goethe said, 'Whatever you can do or dream, you can, begin it. Boldness has genius, magic and power in it. Begin it now.'

My Dream

Impossible, they said.
A miracle, my dream,
a vision for ten years.
Halls of learning,
hallowed buildings,
my old stamping ground
a decade ago.
Vision unfaded,
perpetual student
thriving on learning.
Impossible, they said.
Brain injury extreme.
Cat scans – no hope.
Miracle from God not man.
Knowledge, music,
like heavenly manna
feeding the soul.
Impossible, they said.
Why not? Prove yourself.
University unquestionable.
Acceptable, encouraging,
my plea acknowledged.

Refreshing, participating,
doubting, believing I can.
Impossible, they said.
Fight for survival
in an erudite world.
Pathways of success.
I, like thousands before me,
strive, overcome, not yielding.
A miracle has begun.

20 April 2002

My years at university 2002–2011

The journey to my Masters began when I returned to Adelaide University in March 2002. I was asked to do a refresher year so I chose music theory. Alan Mills was the lecturer, and he impressed me very much. He was an American with a good knowledge of Bach and a dry sense of humour. I liked him a lot. We studied baroque music and he made it come alive. I enjoyed his lectures and writing his assignments. My best effort was my two-part invention. I dictated it by writing to Mum note by note so she could write it on the manuscript for me. It took a long time as you can imagine. It is in the style of J.S. Bach, one of my favourite composers.

Airlie's Invention

In the second semester, we had Graeme Dudley and Graeme Koehne. The period was twentieth-century music. I didn't enjoy this as much, because we studied so many different styles. I don't like Webern, but my twelve-tone composition was my best result, apart from the listening exam. Overall, I received a distinction and I was very happy.

The two Graemes with 'e's lectured in tandem. They were conspicuous by their absence sometimes and we also had Stephen Whittington, who filled in a few times. Graeme Koehne was the best lecturer of the three.

In 2003, I started Honours BMus in Musicology. I was lucky enough to be assisted this year by a grant from the Sir Charles Bright Scholarship Fund, and I was very grateful for this help. To complete this two-year project, I had to write four essays and one exegesis. I really wanted to do them all on opera, my great love, but my tutor, Professor Charles Bodman Rae, advised me otherwise. My topics were discussions about Beethoven Sonata op. 110; a discussion of and comparison of *Parzival* (Eschenbach) and *Parsifal* (Wagner); Debussy's *The Submerged Cathedral* and *Pagodas*; and a comparison of the Japanese aspects of a Noh drama *Sumidagawa* with *Curlew River*, an opera by Benjamin Britten. For my exegesis, I wrote an argument debating that *Parsifal*, the opera by Wagner, is not a Christian work. My topic was 'Wherein lies the magic and religious or Christian symbolism of Good Friday' (Act III). I must thank Dr Brian Dickey, a friend from church, for giving me excellent encouragement for and feedback on this piece of writing.

Airlie Jane Kirkham BA Graduate Diploma Secondary Education, BMus (Hons).

I graduated with class 2A Honours in Musicology in 2005.

AGAINST THE ODDS: Airlie Kirkham with her parents, Pamela and Les, after receiving her Masters degree and, above, in 1990 when she graduated with a Bachelor of Music. **Main picture:** Sam Wundke

From the Sunday Mail, 14 August 2005 – note it should read 'Honours degree'. (Photo by Sam Wundke)

Graduation Day

My dream is real.
The day has come
to give me honour
and success.
It was an impossible dream of long ago,
No way, they said,
but defying the odds
I trod a steady path forward.
Admittedly it took longer
than for those who walk on feet,
while I who walk on wheels
rolled slowly on.
Hard work, much reading,
more writing, but I did not
give up.
Now the time draws near.
What honours will I get?

I have proved my critics wrong.
I have succeeded
with the help of my right hand,
my mother, who stood by me
and encouraged from behind.
Resplendent in cap and gown,
bright green and black hood,
I will not forget this day.
Honours Musicology,
my heart's desire.

August 2005

I took ill in the latter part of 2005 and this set me back considerably for six months. Undaunted, I applied for Master of Music study for 2006, after I had fully recovered. I was awarded a university scholarship to do the research for this project. This Masters by research took me nearly five years to complete part-time.

Associate Professor Dr Kimi Coaldrake was my postgraduate coordinator. She was a very caring and supportive person throughout my candidature. Kimi introduced me to the graphic tablet connected to my laptop. This enabled me to record my writings for the thesis using a stylus in a more practical and quicker way.

Professor Charles Bodman Rae, Elder Professor, was one of my tutors. He was kind and gentle, and sought ways to ensure that I was successful. At our first interview, he said to me, 'I have not come here to tell you whether you can do your Masters, but rather, how you can do it and go about this task to be successful.' I had been really worried about it all up till that point. Charles recognised that I had perfect pitch and suggested I should utilise this skill to my best advantage. Therefore I chose to analyse selected performances of six sopranos and four tenors aurally.

In my first year, I wrote the core component structured program (CCSP) and presented it in class on 26 October 2006. My other tutor, Associate Professor Dr Mark Carroll, read it for me, and I answered questions using my newly acquired graphic tablet and laptop computer.

The research proposal development was one of the hardest parts. When I tried to write the thesis in the following year, I found I had some difficulties. I needed to amend my topic, after much frustration in trying to make my aim and direction clear.

Once I wrote the topic more clearly, it was much easier to sit down and write each chapter. I wrote my thesis in a different way from normal research, by focusing on aural analysis and interpretation. My topic was 'An aural analysis of bel canto: Traditions and interpretations as preserved through selected sound recordings'.

I have always loved opera and over many years I have read books on opera. I have held the tradition of bel canto in high regard because of its natural purity and use of the voice. The operas of Puccini, Bellini and Donizetti have provided me with many memorable occasions. My most memorable and particular performance was in the summer of 1987 when Placido Domingo sang the leading role in *La Bohème* (Puccini) in Covent Garden.

It is obvious why I chose that topic. One of my fellow postgrads, Letho, who was equally passionate about this style of opera, helped me, and encouraged me considerably by lending me videos and tapes from his own collection.

Ode to Letho

> I wonder why I was so lucky,
> for someone, unknown to me at first,
> to stop by me, and express with me
> a love we now share of bel canto opera.
> This was a special time of sharing,
> fortuitous, unplanned, but meant to be.
> A helpmate in a vast wilderness of
> potential providers,
> Amanuensis and encourager.
> How thankful I am.

June 2010

Do not be put off by the frustrations everyone faces at some time during their candidature. My tutors were kind but firm, and I received the same criticisms as any normal student would. It was hard going at times but I was not put off. I just love learning for learning's sake.

It was a long haul, over five years and not without more frustrations and difficulties, but with great support and encouragement from my mother, the university professors, tutors, university researcher education unit and library staff. My 50,000-word thesis was finally finished. It was a great relief, but also a great joy.

The examining process involved submitting three copies soft cover, and three CDs of the music tracks I selected for the aural analysis. I had two unknown examiners, one in Victoria and one in SA. I am so grateful for those who have encouraged me along the way but I did worry about the outcome! I wrote this poem while I was waiting for the results.

Destiny in Master of Music

This is an enigma.
Locked away in two persons
is my destiny,
a mystery, a curiosity.
My mind cannot escape my feelings.
I tried so hard.
All-consuming.
Paper and pen
disseminated my thesis
for what seemed an eternity.
My mind is consumed
with nothing else.
Will I be successful?
May I hope to win
this passion for my life?

June 2010

My examiners were Patrick Power ONZM, MMus (Hons) of the Elder Conservatorium of Music, University of Adelaide, and Emeritus Professor Mel Waters of Melbourne University. They wrote constructive critical reports; one in particular was very helpful in the amount of detail his report contained. Patrick wrote,

> This thesis is a well presented, well referenced, substantial piece of work. The approach is not unique but it is nevertheless uncommon and refreshing. Given the limitations imposed upon the author… it is a remarkable piece of work. It merits the awarding of a degree.

Mel wrote,

> This is an earnest and commendable body of work, and I would encourage the writer to continue to develop her interest, knowledge and understanding of the topic in the future.

I had some corrections to do before I had the final copies printed and bound. The whole process took four months, and after submitting my copies I had confirmation of my results from the graduate centre soon after.

Naturally I had to write a poem about my success.

Master of Music

Words are not enough.
Aural appreciation,
intense listening with an ear on edge,
acutely, purposely,
I play the melody in my mind.
Sounds pitched accurately
determine the outcome.
Opera stars, divas,
the bathroom tenor,
all must strive for perfection.
They are the masters
of style, of pitch, of timbre, of genre,

not the mere observers
who analyse their performances.
A mere mortal becomes a master
by masterful words,
but the true master is the one
who engages the world.

August 2010

I graduated on 31 December 2010 and the presentation ceremony was on 13 April 2011 in Bonython Hall, Adelaide University. University has been the best thing in my life.

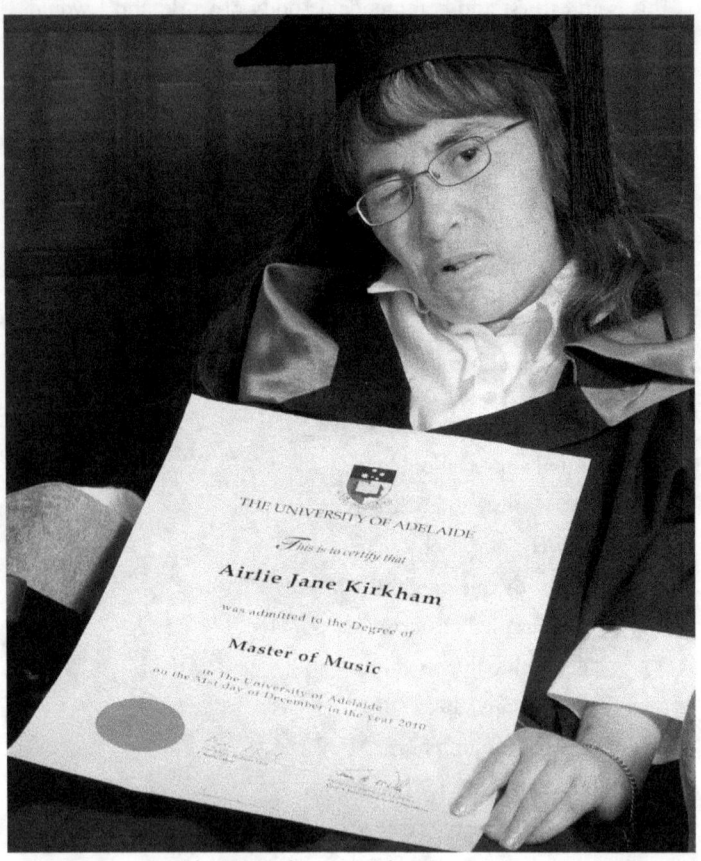

(Photo: Academic Graduation Services)

Epilogue

I want to tell the world that miracles still do happen. God works them in His own time. I want to tell the world to trust in God and to always have hope and belief that a miracle will happen.

I want to tell families never to give up hope, to be strong and determined. These qualities will help them through difficult times. They need to communicate this to their loved one, because even many people in a coma can hear and think. They are sensitive to their environment and need to be aware of their family's strong hope and faith in them.

My situation has often seemed intolerable. I still cannot walk, talk and eat properly. I need a daily team of dedicated carers to help me in all aspects of daily life. But I have been sustained by all the loving people around me.

Above all, I want to tell my family that I love them dearly, and I will be grateful to them forever, for standing by me in such a tragic situation. I want to talk to them every day and tell them I love them. They have suffered as much as me in a different way, but they are strong and have great faith in God, which has encouraged and supported me.

I step forward in faith daily. I trust in God to see me through this situation wherever he takes me. There is no other way.

> I know His peace,
> His loving arms around me,
> I will be content.

There is light at the end of the tunnel, but one has to find the way there. I have found that light and, with God's help, it will lead me on into the future.

www.ingramcontent.com/pod-product-compliance
Lightning Source LLC
Chambersburg PA
CBHW062149100526
44589CB00014B/1748